GIANT ANIMALS

WHALE SHARKS

Rebecca Stefoff

Cavendish
Square

New York

Published in 2015 by Cavendish Square Publishing, LLC
243 5th Avenue, Suite 136, New York, NY 10016

Library of Congress Cataloging-in-Publication Data

Stefoff, Rebecca, 1951- author.
Whale sharks / Rebecca Stefoff.
pages cm. — (Giant animals)
Includes bibliographical references and index.
ISBN 978-1-62712-954-1 (hardcover) ISBN 978-1-62712-956-5 (ebook)
1. Whale shark—Juvenile literature. I. Title.

QL638.95.R4S74 2015
597.3'3—dc23

2013050647

Editorial Director: Dean Miller
Editor: Andrew Coddington
Copy Editor: Wendy Reynolds
Art Director: Jeffrey Talbot
Designer: Joseph Macri
Photo Researcher: J8 Media
Production Manager: Jennifer Ryder-Talbot
Production Editor: David McNamara

The photographs in this book are used by permission and through the courtesy of: Cover photo by Joanne Weston/Shutterstock.com; Brian J. Skerry / National Geographic/Getty Images, 4; © B.A.E. Inc./Alamy, 6; Mary Evans/Natural History Museum/age fotostock, 8; Reid, Rich/Animals Animals, 9; © Michael Patrick O'Neill/Alamy, 10; Ross Armstrong/age fotostock, 13; Jason Edwards/National Geographic/Getty Images, 14; Dorling Kindersley/ Dorling Kindersley RF/Thinkstock, 16; AFP/Stringer/AFP/Getty Images, 17; © Cathleen Bester, 19; © Watt, Jody/Animals Animals, 20; © Cranston, Bob/Animals Animals, 22; Ross Armstrong/age fotostock, 22; © Watt, Jody/Animals Animals, 23; Ross Armstrong/ age fotostock, 25; Luis Javier Sandoval Alvarado/Science Faction/Getty Images, 26; © Franklin Viola/Animals Animals, 28; Cranston, Bob/ Animals Animals, 30; Reinhard Dirscherl/Tips Images RM/age fotostock, 31; © Watt, Jody/Animals Animals, 32; Paul Sutherland/National Geographic/Getty Images, 34; © Andre Seale/Specialist Stock RM/age fotostock, 35; Gianluca Colla/National Geographic/ Getty Images, 36; paul cowell photography/Flickr/Getty Images, 39; Rex Features via AP Images, 40; Imaginechina via AP Images, 41.

Printed in the United States of America

CONTENTS

CHAPTER ONE

THE BIGGEST FISH IN THE SEA

Don't be fooled by the name. The whale shark is not a whale. But it is a shark—the biggest shark in the world.

The whale shark isn't just the world's biggest shark, it is also the world's biggest fish. Millions of years ago, however, sharks even larger than today's whale sharks swam the seas.

The First Sharks

Whale sharks belong to an ancient group of animals: fish. Fish have been around for more than 500 million years. This means it has been half a billion years since fish appeared. They were the first animals to have skeletons. They moved through the water by bending their flexible, scale-covered bodies and steering with their fins.

By 420 million years ago there were many different **species**, or kinds, of fish. They fell into two main groups. One group had skeletons made of bone. The other group had skeletons made of a tough, rubbery material called **cartilage**. Humans have ears and noses made of cartilage, but our skeletons are mostly bone. For the cartilage fish, it was the other way around. Their skeletons were made entirely of cartilage, but some parts, especially their jaws and spines, built up layers of calcium and other minerals that gave them the hardness of bone.

Some of these fish left parts of their bodies behind, which then were turned to stone in the form of **fossils**. A fossil is an ancient plant or animal that has kept its original shape, sometimes for hundreds of millions of years. That's because, over time, bones and other materials from living things can be replaced by minerals from the soil or water. This process of fossilization lets modern scientists study many samples of early life.

Scales, teeth, and jaws from cartilage fish became fossils. So did some of the thicker parts of their skeletons, such as pieces of their backbones. From these fossils, scientists have pieced together pictures of one group of early cartilage fish—the first sharks.

The oldest definite evidence of sharks comes from fossil scales that are about 420 million years old. Experts agree that these scales are from sharks because they have the same tooth-like shape as the scales of modern sharks. Some scientists think that even older scales, from

The fossil of an ancient shark shows the shape of its head, spine, and fins, preserved in stone.

about 455 million years ago, came from sharks, but other experts do not agree. Still, at 420 million years ago, sharks were around long before dinosaurs or mammals existed.

Starting around 380 million years ago, the fossil record holds more shark remains, including teeth, spines, jaws, and skulls. One of the oldest sharks known from these fossils is called Antarctilamna. It became extinct ages ago, but its remains have been found in Antarctica, Australia, and Saudi Arabia—lands that were once the bottoms of ancient seas.

Many families and species of sharks **evolved** and then became extinct, replaced by new species. At first, sharks were abundant in the world's oceans. They were **predators** that lived and hunted close to shore, in shallow waters. Then, around 250 million years ago, a mass extinction killed off more than 90 percent of all species of ocean life, along with about 70 percent of all land species. Scientists are still looking for the explanation for this "Great Dying." The species that survived gave rise to new families of living things. Some sharks survived the Great Dying and became the ancestors of new varieties of sharks.

By 200 million years ago the age of dinosaurs had begun. It was around then that the first modern shark families appeared. The shark species that lived at that time are now extinct, but modern sharks are descended from some of them. Those early ancestors of today's sharks were predators that lived and hunted fairly close to shore. But by 100 million years ago, many shark species had developed a new way of life. They became swift-swimming hunters that prowled deeper waters, farther from shore. Sharks were becoming predators of the whole ocean.

Megalodon: Biggest Shark Ever

For millions of years, the ancient seas were home to a super-sized relative of today's great white shark. It is called Megalodon, which means "giant tooth." The name is no exaggeration. Fossil Megalodon teeth can measure as much as 7 inches (18 centimeters) from top to bottom, compared with about 3 inches (8 cm) for the biggest great white shark teeth.

An average great white shark is about 15 feet (4.5 meters) long when fully grown, but Megalodon could reach lengths of 60 feet (18 m) or more, making it the largest shark known to ever have existed. Scientists think that it preyed on ancient species of enormous whales. Megalodon lived in all the world's oceans, starting about 20 million years ago. This massive predator must have been king of the prehistoric seas, but around 2 million years ago, it became extinct.

Compare the tooth of a great white shark (on right) to a Megalodon tooth (on left). Megalodon could easily gobble up the biggest great white.

Dinosaurs and many other forms of life disappeared during another mass extinction around 65 million years ago. Some families of sharks survived, and one of those families evolved into a new group of sharks.

Instead of being predators that hunted and fed on other fish, this new group ate much smaller prey, such as the tiny sea creatures called **plankton**. Scientists call these new sharks **filter feeders** because they filtered seawater across special tooth-like structures in their bodies. The structures trapped the plankton, which the sharks could then swallow. In this way, the filter feeders ate millions of very small animals instead of hunting and killing large prey.

Plankton, made up of millions of tiny creatures, swirls in the clear waters off a Mexican beach.

Sharks Today

There are between 440 and 500 species of sharks alive today. The number is not exact for two reasons. First, new shark species are discovered from time to time. Second, scientists sometimes disagree about how to define a species, especially if only a few samples of it have been found.

Scientists generally divide modern sharks into eight groups, called orders. Each order contains one or more smaller groups called families, and each family contains one or more species. Basking sharks, megamouth sharks, mako sharks, and great white sharks, for example, are part of an order called mackerel sharks. Hammerhead sharks, bull sharks, and tiger sharks belong to a different order, ground sharks.

Sharks' closest relatives are a large group of fish that also have skeletons made of cartilage. These are the rays and skates—broad, flat fish that skim along above the sea floor. More than 500 species of rays and skates are known. Some of them, such as manta rays, are filter feeders that eat plankton. Others eat clams, snails, and smaller fish.

The Atlantic guitarfish is a ray, a relative of the sharks. Rays and skates are sometimes called "flat sharks."

Whale Sharks and Their Relatives

If you think of sharks as deadly hunters and fierce killers, you may be surprised to learn that the whale shark does not hunt at all. That's right—the biggest shark in the world is not a predator. It is a filter feeder.

Whale sharks belong to an order called carpet sharks. The name comes from the fact that many of the sharks in this order have patterns of spots and sometimes stripes on their backs, giving them the look of a patterned rug or carpet.

There are forty or so species of carpet sharks in seven families. These families are nurse sharks, bamboo sharks, collared carpet sharks, blind sharks (which are not really blind), the wobbegongs (an Australian name), the zebra shark (the only species in its family), and the whale shark (also the only species in its family).

Most carpet sharks live in the warm waters around Indonesia, Australia, and the shores of the eastern Pacific Ocean. They drift along close to the ocean floor. Although some carpet sharks live at depths of up to 600 feet (180 m), many are usually found at 200 feet (60 m) or so, or in even shallower waters around reefs. There the patterned backs of the carpet sharks provide camouflage. The patterns break up the sharks' outlines and help them blend into the seafloor pattern of light and shadow, rock and sand.

The big exception is the whale shark. Unlike all the other carpet sharks, it is not a bottom dweller. Although whale sharks spend some time in shallow waters not far from shore, they are at home in the open sea.

In addition to patterned backs, whale sharks share a few other features with the rest of the carpet sharks. Close to their mouths are sense organs called **barbels**, which look like short whiskers or tentacles. The barbels are taste buds that help the sharks locate food. All carpet sharks have two fins on their backs and five **gill** slits—openings through which water passes when the shark breathes—on their sides. (Most other kinds of sharks have five gill slits as well, but a few species have seven.)

There is a lot of variety in the carpet shark order. The diet of these sharks ranges from fish to clams and lobsters to squid and coral, depending on the species. The whale shark is the only filter feeder in the order. Like their diet, the size of carpet sharks covers a broad range. The smallest known member of the order is the barbelthroat carpet shark, which measures 13 inches (33 cm) or so in length. The biggest carpet shark is forty times longer than the barbelthroat. That giant of the modern seas is the whale shark.

A large whale shark's mouth is about five feet wide, but its throat is only a few inches across.

CHAPTER TWO

INSIDE THE WHALE SHARK'S SKIN

From their skins to their stomachs, from their snouts to their tails, whale sharks are built for life in the sea. In many ways they are like all other shark species. In other ways, such as their huge size, they are unique. To understand the life of a whale shark, it helps to know something about its **anatomy,** or physical structure.

The Shape of a Shark

Sharks generally have a streamlined body shape that can move quickly through the water. Their bodies are sometimes called "torpedo-shaped," which means that they are long, smooth, and tapered, like the under-water missiles called torpedoes.

The whale shark does not fit this pattern. While most sharks have long, narrow heads that end in pointed snouts, the whale shark does not. Instead, its head is wide, with a broad, blunt snout. The shape of the whale shark's head means that it cannot cut through the water as fast as most other species. However, because the whale shark does not

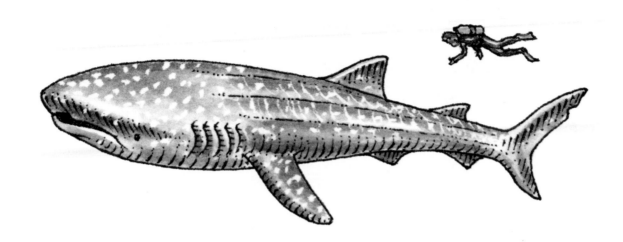

Whale sharks are gentle giants of the sea, even though they are much larger than human divers.

hunt, it does not have to swim as fast or move as nimbly as sharks that are predators.

Whale sharks and all other sharks drive themselves forward through the water by bending their bodies sideways. Their snouts and tails curve first to one side, then to the other. Whipping their tails from side to side gives them speed. The blue shark, a predator with a narrow, pointed snout, can swim in short bursts at speeds of 40 miles (65 kilometers) an hour. Whale sharks are slow swimmers, moving at an average speed of about 3 miles (5 km) an hour. Even large hunting sharks, though, usually cruise along slowly.

A shark's body is basically a tube with fins. Like almost all other sharks, whale sharks have eight fins in all. The two pectoral fins stick out sideways, one on either side of the body. The first and second dorsal fins stand up from the top of the shark's back. The two pelvic fins stick down from its underside. Behind the pelvic fins is a single, smaller anal fin. The eighth fin is the caudal fin at the end of the tail. The caudal fin is usually shaped like a V or a C, and it includes two sections called lobes. One lobe points up, the other down.

The pectoral fins are flat and fairly stiff. Sharks change the angle of their pectoral fins to steer themselves upward or downward as they swim. Some sharks, including whale sharks, also have stiff ridges called keels along their sides, near their tails. Keels help keep whale sharks stable, or balanced, in the water.

Skin and Scales

A whale shark's skin has two layers. The inner layer is the **dermis**. It contains muscles, blood vessels, and nerve cells that are part of the shark's sense of touch. The outer, protective layer is the **epidermis**. The whale shark has the thickest skin of any shark. Its dermis and epidermis together can be as much as 6 inches (15 cm) thick.

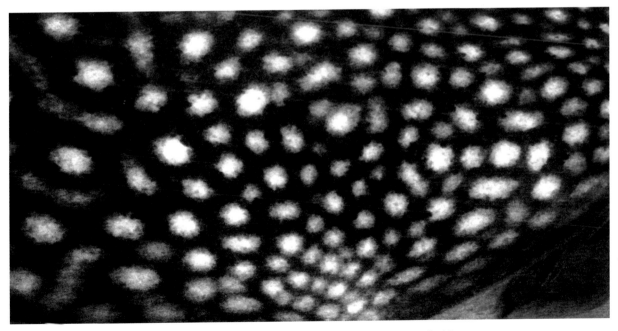

Like all fish in the carpet shark order, whale sharks have patterned skin.

On sharks, the epidermis is covered with special cells called **dermal denticles.** These are the shark's scales. Unlike the scales of bony fish, shark scales are like small teeth. In fact, they are made out of the same strong materials as teeth—dentine with a hard outer shell of enamel.

The size and shape of a shark's denticles varies from species to species. Bramble sharks have sharp, thorn-shaped denticles. Whale shark denticles are flat and plate-like. The denticles overlap each other, and each one has ridges, or keels, running from front to back on its upper surface. The whale shark's overlapping, ridged scales help its huge body move through the ocean by breaking down water resistance into many small streams flowing along the shark's body.

Senses

Whale sharks and other sharks have the same five senses that humans have: sight, hearing, smell, taste, and touch. They also have some sense organs that are special to fish.

Scientists do not know enough about whale sharks to know what sense they use most. They do know that smell is highly important to many shark species. Water flows into two nostrils on the shark's snout, and then across cells that are sensitive to chemicals in the water. Those cells send signals to a section of the shark's brain that interprets them as scents.

Predatory sharks rely on their keen senses of smell to locate prey. They are especially good at scenting blood or body fluids from a wounded or injured animal in the water. Whale sharks are not hunters, and it is not clear how much they rely on scent when they are feeding. But hunting is not a shark's only use for its sense of smell.

Lots of Little Teeth

A close-up of whale shark teeth. Each tooth is about a quarter of an inch long.

Ever since the movie *Jaws*, sharks have been notorious for their huge, sharp teeth. Whale sharks' teeth are sharp, but they are also tiny—only .25 inches (.6 cm) long. There are a lot of them, however. Whale sharks have about 300 rows of teeth in both their upper and lower jaws, and about 3,000 teeth altogether.

Whale sharks don't bite, so why do they have teeth? Scientists think that the teeth are relics from the distant past, left over from a time when the ancient ancestors of whale sharks were predators. As one family of sharks evolved over a long period of time to become filter feeders, their teeth became less and less necessary, and slowly they grew smaller and smaller. The result is the whale shark of today, with its tiny teeth. If whale sharks survive far into the future, their teeth may someday disappear entirely.

Chemical trails and traces in the water help sharks navigate, or find their way around, and also find and communicate with other sharks of their own species.

Like all carpet sharks, whale sharks have dangling, whiskerlike barbels near their mouths. These barbels have taste buds on them. The other species of carpet sharks search for prey in the mud, sand, and weeds of the sea floor, using their barbels to locate prey by tasting it. The barbels of the whale shark, which does not feed on the sea floor, are very small. They may be left over, like the whale shark's teeth, from the distant past when the ancestors of whale sharks had feeding habits like those of the other carpet sharks.

In general, sharks have good eyesight. Their eyes are located on the sides of their heads, which gives the sharks a big field of view to see what is going on around them. Species that live in deep water often have large eyes, which allow them to gather as much light as possible in the dim depths. Whale sharks, which live near the surface, have eyes that are small in relation to their great body size.

Small eyes for a big body.

Sound travels through water, and sharks are equipped with ears. Unlike human ears, though, a shark's ears are completely inside its head. Water enters two small ear-holes behind the eyes. Inside the ears are delicate cartilage tubes full of fluid, as well as small, stone-like objects called otoliths. The movements of the liquid and the otoliths give the shark its sense of direction and motion. Sound waves are picked up by the otoliths, too.

Like some other kinds of fish, sharks have another sense organ called a lateral line. It is a small tube or tunnel under the shark's skin, running from its head to its tail on each side. Water enters the tube through tiny holes and flows across fine, hair-like sense cells. Based on the motion of water inside the lateral-line tube, the sense cells communicate information about what is going on around the shark. Hundreds of tiny vibrations, currents, and flows tell the shark that a prey animal is thrashing nearby, for example, or that a boat or a bigger fish is approaching.

Sharks are also aware of electrical fields in the water through a sense called **electroreception**. All living animals produce small amounts of electricity when they use their muscles. Sharks sense these electrical fields with special sense organs called **ampullae of Lorenzini**. The ampullae are tiny openings dotted around the shark's snout. Inside the openings are sense cells similar to the ones in the shark's ears and lateral lines. In the ampullae, these cells pick up electrical signals. Together with the other senses, electroreception helps a shark locate prey. Hunting sharks can have as many as 1,500 ampullae. Bottom-feeding sharks and whale sharks have just a few hundred.

Gills and Breathing

Like all animals, sharks need oxygen to live. Fish get their oxygen from water, using special structures called gills that are located along their throats. Gills are C-shaped pieces of cartilage, called gill arches,

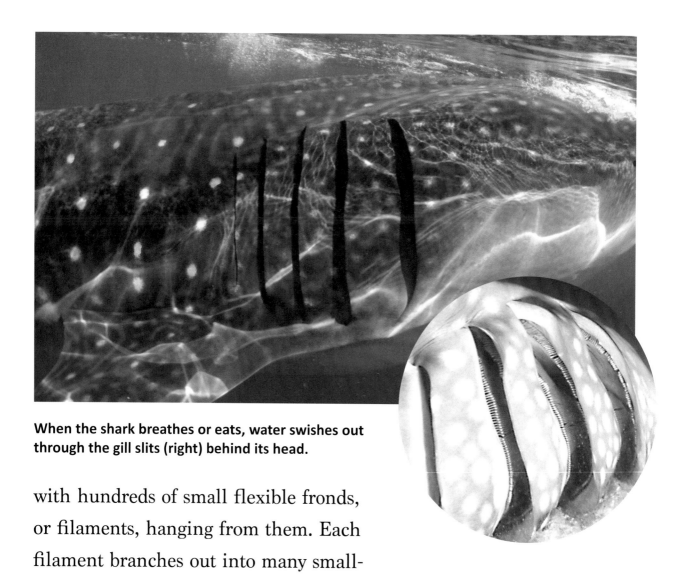

When the shark breathes or eats, water swishes out through the gill slits (right) behind its head.

with hundreds of small flexible fronds, or filaments, hanging from them. Each filament branches out into many small-er filaments full of tiny blood vessels called capillaries. The walls of the capillaries are made of cells so thin that chemicals such as oxygen can pass through them from the water into the blood. The feathery structure of the filaments creates a lot of surface area for water to flow across capillary walls.

A shark "breathes" the water that enters its mouth. The water then flows across the gills. The capillaries in the filaments absorb oxygen, and then the water flows out of the shark's body through the gill slits, the openings in its sides, behind its head.

Water can enter a shark's mouth in two ways. A shark can suck water into its mouth, and then close its mouth to force the water back across the gills and out the slits. Most sharks, including whale sharks, breathe this way. Some fast-moving sharks, however, don't have to suck in water. They swim with their mouths open, scooping in enough water to provide the oxygen they need.

Shark species that spend a lot of time on the sea floor, resting or slowly feeding, have an additional way to breathe in water. They have spiracles, which are small openings behind their eyes. Water enters the spiracles and flows across the gills and out the gill slits. Sharks' close relatives, the rays and skates, are bottom dwellers, and they also have spiracles.

Whale sharks can breathe in two ways: either by swimming with their mouths open or by sucking water in through their mouths.

Internal Organs

Like other animals, sharks have blood that carries oxygen and nutrients to their cells and also removes waste from the cells. Blood is moved through the body by the heart, a strong muscle that lies behind the shark's lower jaw. The heart contracts, or squeezes, to pump out blood through a large blood vessel called the ventral aorta. The aorta divides into branches of smaller capillaries that absorb oxygen and nutrients and carry them around the body. The shark's tissues absorb the oxygen and nutrients through the capillary walls. With its oxygen and nutrients used up, the blood returns to the heart through a series of different vessels, the veins, and then the heart pumps it out again.

Two organs called the kidneys are the main part of the shark's waste-disposal system. Blood collects waste products from the tissues and deposits them in the kidneys. Liquid waste from the kidneys and solid waste from the stomach both leave the shark's body through the same opening, the cloaca, which is near the anal fin.

The liver is the biggest organ in the shark's body. It contains an oil called squalene, which contains high amounts of vitamins A and D. Squalene is lighter than water. This gives the shark **buoyancy**, meaning that it helps keep the shark from sinking.

Buoyancy

The body of a shark is a little heavier than the seawater around it. Without ways to make its body buoyant, the shark would slowly sink. But because the shark's liver is filled with oil that is lighter than water, the liver adds buoyancy and prevents the shark from sinking. Whale sharks have large bodies and spend most of their time near the surface of the ocean, so they need a lot of buoyancy. They have large livers, but some experts believe that they add extra buoyancy by swallowing air.

The wing-shaped pectoral fins on the whale shark's sides also help keep the shark from sinking under its own weight. As the shark moves forward, its fins act like airplane wings, adding lift and raising the front of the body so that the snout points upward instead of downward. If the shark stops moving forward, however, its oil-filled liver alone does not give it enough buoyancy to keep it from drifting downward. For this reason sharks remain in constant motion, unless they are resting on the ocean bottom.

Scientists do not know how much time whale sharks spend on the bottom of the ocean, if any. Whale sharks do have **spiracles**. These are usually found in bottom-dwelling fish, but the massive whale sharks are believed to spend most of their lives swimming on or near the ocean's surface—although in 2009, researchers reported that a whale shark they had been studying had dived to more than 4,000 feet

Small carpet sharks spend most of their time on or near the ocean bottom, unlike the whale shark.

(1,220 m) below the surface. Many details about the life and habits of the whale shark are yet to be discovered.

CHAPTER THREE

THE LIFE OF THE WHALE SHARK

Humans have marveled at whale sharks since at least the year 1828. That's when a military doctor named Andrew Smith examined and measured a huge fish that had been harpooned in Table Bay, at the southern tip of Africa. That fish was a little over 15 feet long (4.5 m), much smaller than the largest whale sharks that have been seen and measured since then. Still, Smith was impressed by the size of the fish, which he recognized as a shark. He called it a "whale shark" because of its size—it was a whale of a shark—and also because it had a big, wide, blunt head like some species of whales.

Smith was the first person to publish a scientific description of the whale shark, although the species was already known to sailors and fishing people in many parts of the world. He chose the whale shark's scientific name. It is *Rhincodon typus*, which means "rasp-toothed type." The name refers to the whale shark's many small, sharp teeth, which are like the teeth of the tool known as a rasp.

Almost two centuries have passed since Andrew Smith measured that big fish on a South African beach. During that time, scientists have found answers to some of their questions about the whale shark, but many parts of this super-sized shark's life remain a mystery.

How Big Is the Biggest Living Shark?

The largest whale shark ever measured scientifically was 41.5 feet (12.5 m) long. It weighed about 47,000 pounds (21,300 kilograms). Divers and people who work on fishing boats have reported seeing whale sharks as long as 60 feet (18 m). These claims are not proven, but some of the experts who have studied whale sharks think it is possible that some individuals reach such lengths. If so, there may be whale sharks alive today that match the extinct giant Megalodon in size.

Even at 41.5 feet (12.5 m), the whale shark is definitely the biggest fish in the sea today. But it isn't the biggest creature in the sea. That honor goes to a mammal: the blue whale. At up to 100 feet (30 m) long, weighing as much as 400,000 pounds (181,500 kg), blue whales are not just the largest animals alive today, they are also the largest known animals that have ever lived on Earth.

A snorkeler cruises above a whale shark in Australian waters. Whale sharks are not predators, but human swimmers should avoid disturbing them.

Filter Feeding

Some species of whales are filter feeders—including the largest whale, the blue whale, and other big species such as the fin, bowhead, right, and humpback whales. These filter-feeding whales have plates in their mouths from which hang strands of stiff bristles called baleen. The baleen acts like a net or strainer, filtering small food items out of the water.

The whale shark is a filter feeder, too, but it uses a different mechanism. Each of its gill arches has two filter pads. In most fish, the gill arches have stiff plates or pads called gill rakers that block large objects that could hurt the fish's ability to absorb oxygen from flowing across the gill filaments and through the gill slits. But in whale sharks, the gill rakers have evolved into filter pads that are covered with dermal denticles, like hundreds of tiny teeth or scales. The filter pads strain even very small objects out of the water.

For whale sharks, feeding means taking in large quantities of water, then filtering out the food items in the water. The shark can take in water in two ways: scooping it or sucking it. Either way, the first step is opening its mouth.

The whale shark's mouth looks small when it is closed and viewed from the side. But when the mouth is open, seen from the front, it is enormous. The gaping mouth stretches forward like the nozzle of a huge vacuum cleaner. The shark either scoops water in by swimming forward, or sucks it in like a person drawing in a deep breath. When the shark closes its mouth, the water is pushed over the filter pads and on through the gills, where oxygen passes from the water into the blood. Meanwhile, the food trapped on the filter pads moves on down the throat to the stomach. If necessary, the whale shark can clear clogged food from its filter pads with a movement like a cough.

Two other species of sharks are filter feeders. They are the basking shark and the megamouth shark. Unlike the whale shark, which is a member of the carpet shark order, they belong to the mackerel shark order. And, while scientists think that the whale shark uses the suction method of feeding most of the time, these two types of shark feed only by scooping water into their mouths as they swim.

A whale shark can suck huge amounts of plankton-filled water into its enormous mouth.

Whale sharks have been seen moving their heads from side to side as they feed, like someone using a vacuum cleaner to sweep up crumbs. Whale sharks have also been observed "standing up" to eat—hanging vertically in the water with their heads aimed at the surface, bobbing up and down as they gulp mouthfuls of food-bearing water.

The whale shark's diet is usually described as "plankton," but that term can cover many different kinds of creatures, from bacteria to fish eggs, jellyfish, and the larvae of crabs and fish. Any of the many kinds of sea life—mostly very small—that drift with the current instead of swimming on their own can be called plankton. Whale sharks also eat krill, which are small, shelled, plankton-eating creatures related to shrimp. In addition, whale sharks have been known to eat larger items, such as fish and squid. Scientists do not know whether the whale sharks seek out this larger prey or simply suck it in along with the seawater.

Whale sharks sometimes eat food larger than plankton. This Indonesian shark is inhaling small fish.

Spots, Stripes, and Surface Swimmers

The upper side of a whale shark is dark, ranging from brownish to blue-gray. Its underside is white. This coloration is found on many sharks and other fish. It is called countershading. Scientists think that countershading evolved to make fish harder to spot. If seen from below, the pale underside helps the fish blend into the background of light at the surface. If seen from above, the dark upper body helps it blend into the background of darkness below.

Whale sharks' upper bodies are not just dark. They are covered with patterns of pale, whitish stripes and spots. Each whale shark has its own unique pattern. These markings are so distinctive that they can be used to identify individual sharks, just as fingerprints are used to identify individual people.

Carpet sharks got their name because of their patterned markings. Those markings provide camouflage for species of carpet sharks that live close to the sea bottom. What use are the markings to the whale shark, which is not a bottom dweller? One possible explanation is that the stripes and spots mimic the rippling patterns of light on the waves at the ocean's surface, giving the whale shark protective coloration.

Each whale shark's pattern is as unique as a human fingerprint.

Life Cycle

Whale sharks have been found around the globe, usually in the warmer waters on either side of the Equator. In the Atlantic Ocean they have been seen from the coast of Brazil to as far north as New York. Many sightings of whale sharks happen in the Gulf of Mexico, the waters off Mexico's west coast, the tropical Pacific Ocean, Southeast Asia, and the Indian Ocean.

Whale sharks are known to gather at certain times of the year near the island nation of Taiwan in the Eastern Pacific, the northern Philippines, and Australia's Ningaloo Reef. Scientists think that the whale sharks come to feed on giant population explosions, or blooms, of plankton in those locations. Experts who study whale sharks are learning that the sharks migrate over long distances, swimming from one good feeding ground to another.

One research method involves attaching tags with electronic signals to whale sharks, and then tracking the sharks' movement using satellites. This method has shown that whale sharks regularly cover long distances, such as the two-month, 1,250-mile (2,000 km) journey from the Philippines to the sea south of Vietnam, or the 37-month, 8,100-mile (13,000 km) journey from the west coast of Mexico to the Pacific island nation of Tonga.

Whale sharks are often seen alone, but gatherings of as many as 100 sharks have been recorded. In 2011, researchers reported the largest gathering of whale sharks ever recorded—about 400 of them feeding in the waters off Mexico's Yucatan Peninsula, just south of the Gulf of Mexico.

A researcher attaches a radio tag that will let scientists follow the shark's movements.

The social and family life of whale sharks, if any, is unknown. They have never been observed during courtship or mating. As for producing offspring, some species of sharks release eggs into the water, and others give birth to live pups (the young of all shark species are called pups). Scientists have never seen a female whale shark lay eggs or give birth. Most of their ideas about whale shark reproduction are based on a 36-foot-long (11 m) female whale shark that was harpooned off the coast of Taiwan in the 1990s. Her body contained 307 fetuses in egg sacs.

Experts now think that whale sharks use a type of reproduction called **ovoviviparity**, which is midway between laying eggs and giving birth to live young. The young develop inside egg cases that remain in the mother's body until the pups hatch. At that time, the pups are released into the water. If whale sharks use this method of reproduction, it is possible that not all the eggs hatch at the same time. The female could release the young over a period of days, weeks, or even months.

When whale shark pups begin their free-swimming lives, they are tiny compared with adults of their species. Whale shark pups measuring less than 20 inches (50 cm) in length have been captured.

How long a whale shark lives is another mystery. In general, large animals live longer than small ones. Scientists have come up with different estimates for the average lifespan of whale sharks, from sixty to one hundred years or even more.

As far as scientists know, full-grown whale sharks are seldom preyed upon by other animals. It does happen, however. In 2001 a pair of orcas—also called killer whales—were filmed killing and eating a 24-foot (7.5 m) whale shark. The bodies of smaller, younger whale sharks have been found in the stomachs of predatory fish such as the blue marlin and blue shark.

Scientists have seen scars and bite marks on the bodies of large whale sharks. They do not know whether those marks are the remains of attacks when the whale sharks were younger, or whether some ocean predators occasionally try and fail to eat the slow-moving giants. As with so much else about the whale shark, its relationships with other species of ocean life are not well known. The relationship between whale sharks and the human species, though, is a different matter.

A whale shark pup starts life small and vulnerable to ocean predators.

CHAPTER FOUR

A GENTLE GIANT IN DANGER

One of the many mysteries surrounding the whale shark is how healthy the species is today. Are whale sharks thriving, or just barely surviving? Are there enough whale sharks in the wild to ensure that the species will live on into the future?

Scientists hope that new tools, such as electronic devices to track whale shark migrations and perhaps learn about breeding habits, will help them answer those questions. Meanwhile, **conservationists** (who work to protect the natural world) and **marine** biologists (who study ocean life) are calling for stronger protection for all sharks, including whale sharks.

Whale Sharks and People

Whale sharks are not dangerous to people—although they are huge, and could injure a swimmer or diver who came too close or seemed to threaten the shark. Most of the time when divers encounter whale sharks, the sharks either ignore the divers or swim away. Some divers have positioned themselves above whale sharks and grabbed hold of a dorsal fin to hitch a ride. Marine biologists do not recommend this. As with all wildlife, it is best to leave the animal alone and observe it from a distance.

People are much more dangerous to whale sharks than the other way around. For years, people in many Asian countries, from Pakistan to Taiwan, have fished for whale sharks. The sharks' meat has been eaten by many cultures, although it is most prized in Taiwan and China. Oil from the sharks' liver has been used as a water-resistant coating on wooden fishing boats. In India, for example, fishermen hunted whale sharks with harpoons to get the livers and their oil.

In recent decades, some countries have outlawed the killing of whale sharks, or set limits on how many can be killed. The Maldives, an island nation in the Indian Ocean, began protecting whale sharks in 1995. The Philippines followed in 1998. India banned whale shark fishing in 2001. Taiwan has tried to control the killing of whale sharks by setting an annual limit on the catch. Other nations that have taken legal action to give some protection to whale sharks include Australia, Mexico, Thailand, Malaysia, and Honduras. Whale sharks are protected in the Atlantic Ocean off the coast of the United States.

People are discovering that whale sharks may be worth more alive than dead. The Maldives and the Philippines have led the way with programs to replace fishing with ecotourism. Instead of catching and killing whale sharks, coastal communities have begun offering tours for people who want to see whale sharks in the wild. Western Australia's Ningaloo Reef is another area where whale sharks are protected and tourism is encouraged.

Tourism may prove to be the key to saving the whale shark. It does raise an important question, though: How many tourists can interact with whale sharks—and how close can they get—without harming the sharks or interfering with their natural way of life? There have been reports of whale sharks bumping their heads against tourist boats that came too close.

Trapped in a fisherman's net, the whale shark may be set free. Some nations have laws protecting these giant fish.

Visitors to Australia's Ningaloo Reef hope to see whale sharks during their dive adventure.

In addition to ecotourism opportunities to see whale sharks in the wild, some aquariums around the world are home to live whale sharks. The great size of these fish makes them challenging to keep in captivity, however.

Are Whale Sharks Endangered?

Sharks are in trouble. According to the International Union for Conservation of Nature (IUCN), an organization that monitors the health of thousands of species worldwide, 30 percent of all species of sharks, rays, and skates are endangered. Some

This Soup Is Bad News for Sharks

Each year, people kill millions of sharks. Some are killed for sport, or because they may pose a threat. Some are accidentally caught in nets or on long lines by people fishing for other species. Some are harvested for their meat. But as many as 73 million sharks a year, including whale sharks, are killed for just one thing: their fins, which are used to make a soup that some Asian people regard as a delicacy.

Most of these sharks are killed by the wasteful process of finning, which means slicing the fins from a shark (or a ray) and then throwing the fish back into the sea, either dead or soon to die. To end this practice, conservationists have called for a ban on shark fin soup. But is it fair to ask people to stop eating something that they see as both a tradition and a treat? That question may be hard to answer, but people have given up other foods after they learned more about the animals or formed new ideas about conservation. Only a few cultures today still eat the meat of whales and dolphins, for example. If the whale shark is lucky, shark fin soup will lose its appeal, or possibly be outlawed, and whale sharks and other shark and ray species will keep their fins.

marine biologists and conservationists are calling the situation a shark crisis. They argue that strong international laws to protect sharks are needed.

The whale shark is not an endangered species, according to the IUCN. Based on a shark survey published in 2005, the IUCN labels the whale shark as "vulnerable," which is the level of concern just above "endangered." A vulnerable species is one that could easily be tipped over into endangered status.

At the same time, the IUCN warns that the whale shark population is declining. All evidence suggests that the number of whale sharks in the world's oceans is probably going down. These mighty fish are dying or being killed faster than they can reproduce their numbers.

Sharks have been around for hundreds of millions of years. Whale sharks are not that old—they came on the scene many millions of years after the first sharks appeared. But whale sharks are the largest living members of one of the most ancient kinds of life on Earth. They are creatures of majesty and mystery, gentle giants of the sea. If they become extinct, we will have lost one of the marvels of the planet we all share.

GLOSSARY

ampullae of Lorenzini - sense organs on a shark's snout that pick up electrical fields created by other animals

anatomy - the shape and structure of a living thing and its parts

barbel - sense organ near the mouth that looks like a dangling whisker or short tentacle; acts like a taste bud to help the fish find food

buoyancy - the quality of being able to float or stay at a steady level in water

cartilage - a tough, rubbery substance found in human ears, noses, and parts of the skeleton; bones are made from cartilage that is hardened by deposits of calcium and other minerals

conservationists - people and organizations that work to protect species and habitats

dermal denticles - scales that cover a shark's skin, made of the same material as teeth

dermis - deeper layer of skin, containing blood vessels and nerve cells

electroreception - ability to sense electrical fields

epidermis – surface layer of skin that protects the dermis

evolve – to change slightly from one generation to another; over time, this change, or evolution, creates new species of animals and plants

filter feeder – water-dwelling animal that feeds on plankton and other tiny life forms that it filters, or strains, out of the water

fossil – all or part of an ancient plant or animal, preserved in stone

gill – structure along a fish's throat that absorbs oxygen from water; a fish's organ of breathing

marine – relating to the sea and sea life

ovoviviparity – a method of reproduction in which the young develop inside egg cases within the mother's body and are released alive after they hatch

plankton – forms of sea life, mostly tiny, that drift with the current rather than swimming against it

predator – an animal that lives by killing and eating other animals; a hunter

species – kind of animal or plant; a species includes all the individual animals or plants that can interbreed with each other

spiracle – an opening in the skin of some sharks, near the mouth, for breathing

FIND OUT MORE

Books

Arlon, Penelope. *Sharks.* New York: Scholastic Reference, 2013.

Discovery Channel. *Discovery Channel Sharkopedia: The Complete Guide to Everything Shark.* New York: Time Home Entertainment, 2013.

Hanson, Anders. *Whale Shark.* Minneapolis, MN: SandCastle, 2014.

Nuzzolo, Deborah. *Whale Shark.* Minneapolis, MN: Capstone, 2011.

Websites

Whale Shark

animals.nationalgeographic.com/animals/fish/whale-shark

The National Geographic website features a page of fast facts about the world's largest fish.

Where the Whale Sharks Go

www.npr.org/2013/08/22/214136140/where-the-whale-sharks-go

From National Public Radio, this is a report on new research that may answer questions about the lives of whale sharks.

More Websites

Whale Shark

http://sea.sheddaquarium.org/sea/fact_sheets.asp?id=64

Chicago's Shedd Aquarium offers information about whale sharks, with links to videos and other information.

Mexico: Whale Shark Encounter

video.nationalgeographic.com/video/places/countries-places /mexico/whale-shark-encounter-lex

National Geographic presents a video of divers meeting a whale shark in the ocean off Mexico.

Shark Savers

www.sharksavers.org/en/home

Shark Savers is a nonprofit group working to educate people about sharks, including whale sharks, and also to protect these fish for the future.

INDEX

ABOUT THE AUTHOR

Rebecca Stefoff has published more than a hundred books for young readers. Although she has written about many topics in history and science, writing about biology and nature is one of her specialties. Among her books on animal life is *The Fish Classes* (Cavendish Square, 2008), which explores the evolution and development of the world's fish. A certified scuba diver, Stefoff has explored tropical reefs in Mexico, Central America, the Caribbean, Indonesia, and Hawaii. She has seen sharks on several occasions—but has yet to see her first whale shark in the wild. Stefoff lives in the Pacific Northwest, where she enjoys outdoor activities such as hiking, bicycling, and birding. She now spends more time paddling her kayak on top of the waves than diving beneath them.